THE BULL MURDER

*for Anne
at Great Writing 2017
with love
& best wishes*

PAUL MUNDEN

Paul x

RECENT
WORK
PRESS

The Bulmer Murder
Recent Work Press
Canberra, Australia

Copyright © Paul Munden 2017

National Library of Australia
Cataloguing-in-Publication entry.

Munden, Paul
The Bulmer Murder/ Paul Munden

ISBN: 9780995353824 (paperback)

All rights reserved. This book is copyright. Except for private study, research, criticism or reviews as permitted under the Copyright Act, no part of this book may be reproduced, stored in a retrieval system, or transmitted in any form by any means without prior written permission. Enquiries should be addressed to the publisher.

Cover illustration: Paul Munden, Bulmer Evening
Cover design: Recent Work Press
Set in Adobe Caslon Pro

recentworkpress.com

THE BULMER MURDER

By the same author:

Henderskelfe (with photographs of Castle Howard by Peter Heaton)
Asterisk (with photographs of Shandy Hall by Marion Frith)
Analogue/Digital: New & Selected Poems
Keys (chapbook)
Fire (chapbook)
Feeling the Pressure (editor)

Contents

Tethered	1
Keys	2
Rat Tales	4
Alphabet Jigsaw	11
Molehills	12
Foxed	14
English Pastoral	17
Reprise	18
Ladybirds	20
from The Encyclopædia of Forgotten Things	21
Spiders	24
Brideshead Revisited	26
A Speckled Hen	27
Blackbird	28
A Betrothal	29
Fire	30
The New Slip Inn/The Pub with No Beer	34
Midsummer	36
In a Country Churchyard	37
1768	38
Country House Visitor, c.1996	39
Steadicam	40
All work and no play	41
redruM	42
Macbeth	43
Four Poster	46
Fractures	47
For Sale: Number 453	48
The Bulmer Murder	49
Afterword	62

It takes a hand
to take the hatchet up
and flail that iron
at that flower.

—Pete Morgan, 'The Hatchet & The Rose'

Tethered

Beneath the pantiled roof, joists, rafters,
    insulating foam...

Beneath the humdrum conversation...

Beneath the soft wool pile of the rug...

Beneath the woven seagrass
    bonded to its rubber underlay...

Beneath the concrete screed...

Beneath the visqueen membrane
    keeping down the damp...

Beneath the hardcore, the rubbled brick,
    blinded with sand...

And tethered to a tethering ring of iron
    bolted into bedrock...

A shred of rotting, tethering rope
    grimed with blood

And the muffled squeal that won't let go.

Keys

Clear blue Yorkshire sky. Church done. Potatoes in their goose fat crisping to perfection—you can smell them as the gravel to the front porch crunches underfoot. You wave to the last villager as you turn the key and feel it break: a perforated coin between finger and thumb, useless money, the jagged rest-of-it barreled in the door. The slow dagger of an icicle drips on your head. You rummage in the shed, searching for the thinnest of thin-nosed pliers, your thoughts already turning to broken glass.

*

All around the keyhole, scratches on the brass, and deeper gouges into the surrounding wood, as if the world's worst drunk had made it this far from the Cock and Bull, then lost it big time, howling at the moon. The house is silent as he walks from the flagstoned hallway to the kitchen. He knows what he'll find as he lifts the lid of a massive earthenware jar by the sink. A spare sackful, riddled with weevils, clutters the pantry. He remembers the last outing, thirsty as hell, pulling the lead that now hangs like a streak of blood on the wall.

*

Stripped to your boxers, you try to straighten up and take it on the chin. Why *do* skeletons grin? This one wears a trilby, might as well be smoking a cigar. You watch the articulating bones, sense the response in your own slack spine. The clavicle turns as the doctor lifts one lifeless arm, his voice fading to a whispering drone, and what you overhear, instead, is the time the locum picked up the phone for another opinion—about *a man in his fifties...* You looked around, finding no one else in the room.

*

Equally strange are the old locks, dismembered, in a dusty basket. Excavated mortices: brass casings, levers, springs. Meaningless pieces, their memories shot. The neighbouring jars hold nails, screws, nuts *and* bolts—a rusting semblance of utility. Autumn sunlight slants through cobwebs in the late afternoon, a gentle inquisition. Will anything muster the minimal gleam for a further reprieve? Nothing stirs. Somehow the rumourous groans of misfit futures have been heard—scrapings and squealings that make this silent bedlam a preferable home.

*

He perfected the habit, ducking his head under the keystoned arch. Took pleasure finding everything in its place, blowing dust from the label of just the right wine. He knew the number of apples—each wrapped in newspaper—remaining in the racks. So today, when he grazed his balding scalp, and wiping it, found a smear of blood and lichen on his hand, he shouldn't have been surprised at the paper husks. The empty tray of warfarin. The droppings. The dry roast pork. His wife taking off in a huff.

Rat Tales

Smell a rat,
see a rat,
kill a rat...
Rats is life!

*

A musty smell
lingered
in the air
above the bed.

She stripped
the bedding,
emptied
every drawer,

the wardrobe,
scrubbed every
square inch
of the room

to no effect
and when
she began to peel
the wallpaper

knew that she
had started
to shred
her own mind.

She perched
a ladder
on the landing
to gain access

to the loft,
then lost
her nerve—
summoned

her neighbour
who lifted
the hatch
and shone light

over the pale
yellow lagging
laid between
joists, noted

how the air
was doubly
foul and called
for a shovel.

He lifted strip
after strip,
knowing
what he'd find—

how the body
would look
so much bigger
than imagined

and still haired
as if alive,
so that when
he slid the steel

under its bulk
he half expected
it to writhe
and run at him...

But he held
to his task,
backed his way
down the steps

and dropped
the carcass
on a bonfire
in the garden.

The next day
he returned
to the heap
of warm ash

and saw it:
the perfect skull,
baked white
within the grey.

He knelt, stared
into the space
that was an eye,
and all it took

was the gentlest
tap of his nail
for the collapse
into pure dust.

*

I used to sleep
in the attic
with his baby
and watch

red squirrels
in the oak tree
by the window.
One morning

before I woke
he rushed in
screaming
and I grabbed

the child mere
seconds before
a fat rat ran
around the rim

of the cot, then
onto the bed
and disappeared
under the pillow

where I still
pictured my head
as he battered it
with his spade

again and again
until the shrieks
subsided (and
who knew whose).

*

He took a stroll
round the garden
before turning in,
listening out

for the familiar
owl's soft call
when something
caught his eye—

a luminous cloud
pulsating above
the compost heap,
and as he walked

towards it
the vision seethed
and atomised
into a swarm

of moonlit rats,
robed in white
as if escaped
from an asylum,

and like one, they
turned on him,
fearless,
and he ran.

*

Years later
you still hear
the rusty creak
of the old door

as it opened
onto the smell
of musty corn;
still see—there,

through grainy
half-light
in the corner
of the barn,

from floor
to rafters—
a heavy chain
of rats, nose

to tail, as if
climbing
the twisted rope
of themselves.

*

*And they are all
descended from
Mr and Mrs
Samuel Whiskers,*

*children and great
grandchildren—
there is no
end to them.*

Alphabet Jigsaw

I spread the cut-out shapes
on your bedroom floor
and do my best
to help with the simplest:
a for apple, g for grapes...

but you keep homing in
on r for rainbow
and x—'a sort of photo'
you call *the man with no skin*.

Molehills

Earth crumbles
out of itself, soft
as rumour, building

                        into a friable
                        breathing blot
                        on the lawnscape

        as a helpless
        vagrant, fumbling
        at unreachable air, leaves

                              a trail
                              of poor
                              punctuation...

                blind
                to the spoiled
                vista of manicured grass.

            Insert
            batteries and tap
            home these tapered sonic poles.

                        Warning: moles
                        may at first be attracted
                        through perverse curiosity.

Scrape away
soil to find the hole
then pour in gulps of sump oil

and diesel
until the ground
seals with a repulsive glug;

        try gas—
        the sibilant echo
        of a hushed-up purge

                or light
                a stubby fuse and
                smoke the little fuckers.

    A neighbour
    stands poised
    with an iron spike;

            another
            digs at the speed
            of churning light—reaches

        into the dark
        for one trespasser
        and shuttles to the bottom

of the field,
offering a cruel,
temporary reprieve.

Foxed

1

When he stumbles on the slack wet shape
in the long grass, like something stillborn,
he knows it's his neighbour
who's chucked it there to rot. It's war

that he'll try to refuse as he steps around
the greasy corpse and eyes up
boughs of berried holly within reach
of his shears, sticking to his task.

The last time he walked through the field
the grass was cropped short, bleached
from where the wedding tent had stood.
There were straw bales, still casually placed

for guests long gone, the odd empty bottle
of Black Sheep, and a trail of Love Hearts.

2

He opens the door of the dark compactum
in the bedroom of his childhood home.
Inside, there's a mirror, spotted with rust:
whichever way he looks, his face is fifty years

adrift. There are drawers for shirts, socks,
handkerchiefs, and a tie rack that folds up
flat against the door. He can't see to the back
of the topmost shelf but can feel—

before he reaches it—the small, hard ball
of the nose and the smooth haired
contours of the head. And as he pulls it
from its den, the soft flared brush falls

loose. He wraps it around his shoulders;
fastens the bakelite clasp beneath the jaw.

3

He can taste the fizz of sherbet, still catch
occasional words, looped in purple-pink,
and put a face to every kiss-chased name,
but he remembers, too, how no one

would believe him when he ran in,
breathless, telling his own tale of Mr Tod,
or rather, the hairless cubs he had raced
the wooded length of the drive, at dusk.

Hairless—there was the rub. But he told it
like it was, and even now will not revise
his apparent hallucination as he picks
loose blood-red berries from the basket,

sits by the fire and opens a book, noticing
how the pages match his liver-spotted hands.

English Pastoral

The memory is a silent film—
driving south on a cloistered road
through rich wet Gloucestershire farmland.

At first I hardly noticed them—
each milestone a straw-flecked
                                clod
fallen from the blade
                 of a plough.

Then I saw they were badgers—too many dead
for a coincidence, the cause instead
some savage new cowardice
more self-important than the law, run amok.

I hadn't the stomach
                 to stop and inspect
the gathering flies' sickly critique
of what was rotten, time
                        though to form
my own prejudice.

                 This was England.

                              Now.

Reprise

It starts again, the screeching
early morning practice,
raucous skills brought out
of semi-retirement,
cleaving the rural calm
as if this is all that it's good for
now, a training base for war.

        Maybe you remember it
        from the time your pram
        seemed to rock on its springs
        and your growing wail
        was like the echo of a siren.
        You sense the out-of-nowhere
        wall of colossal sound

and throw yourself to ground
with something close
to justification,
the Tornado
cutting through the air
above your head as it hugs
the contours of the land—

        cornfields rippling
        in its wake—and sucks
        the breath from hill and dale,
        leaving the garden drained
        of colour like a face in shock,
        the world in camouflage:
        re-audible birdsong

so petite;
pastoral light
frail as my father's bones
beneath the hospital sheet;
his voice—mere whisperings
of hard-won reportage...
Butcher Island...

>Yes?... nothing more.
>A bewildered accomplice,
>I scour the map
>for what if anything remains
>and marvel at how you pick
>your small self up
>from your own shadow.

Ladybirds

Wobbling at the top of an aluminium ladder, he sliced through the laurel with his father's shears. Evergreen clippings took off around his face, and from the thick of it, a pigeon, with scissoring wings. Bright drops of blood on the pale green undersides of the leaves he saw were ladybirds, at which he breathed again, but set about his task with greater care, though he was up against time. The sky was darkening. Fat pearls of water gathered on the shrinking hedge like a swarm of little ghosts.

from The Encyclopædia of Forgotten Things

When you hurl the paratrooper from your bedroom window, he hangs for a moment against the sun, making you screw up your eyes. His plastic backpack flips open, the red-white-blue silk billows in the air, and our childhoods linger, conscripted into a slow, slow freefall that matters so much we hold our synchronised breaths… until the crash on gravel—the disjointed figure lying in the yard, staring at the sky—and a silence in which we each expect the other to make some move to retrieve, to try again.

*

Every week, she has trudged the quarter mile to church, taken up her solitary bench, opened the hymn book, and done her best. But every week there is a new fluffed note or erroneous chord that adds to the catalogue of mistakes forgotten by everyone—except her. And today the archival muscle of her fingers has reached its limit. In the shuffling silence as the congregation prepares to draw breath, there's a cracking of joints, and an inexplicable click of her teeth like a malfunctioning machine, followed by nothing.

*

He remembered what must once have been a space, half-cornered by rough stone walls already built, and which a farmer closed in to make a shed. The rotting stable door pulled open and a rusting lamp warmed to its task, casting a glow onto piglets snuggled in straw. He bought it, together with its adjacent house, and when his daughters were born, knocked it all together, turning pigsty to playroom, and watching it acquire its own miniature farmyard, sheep and cows set out on green felt. Later, it was his office, the stone walls cleared to glass, the room reclaiming its infinite borders, while papers and occasional poems thickened its floor.

Putting it to wash, he finds his old maroon t-shirt still holds the ghost of sticky white tape that fixed the electrode to his chest, a fibrous square with a penny-sized absence at its centre somehow meshed to the cotton, even after all these years. He closes the door and watches the machine kick suddenly into reverse—as does the ambulance, taking him back from city hospital to rural dark, its blue light out-blinking the sleepy village. He's slumped at his desk, mumbling answers to questions, questions, watching the empty bottle reacquire its pale orange allure, and feeling the strange jerk of his body twisting the child-proof cap of the plastic container into place. Then there's another kick, a further reverse of the machine, back into the future, saving him from himself.

*

Years after the old stone farmhouse had been sold, and yet another attic was being cleared, there it was, the plywood replica he had crafted in such detail: two staircases, blue patterned wallpaper, and the pale gold carpet, offcut of the real. There were simplifications, of course. The stovepipe in the living room was matt black dowel, but angled in precise correlation to the one that channeled smoke around the high window: that—like all the others—was a square-cut hole, enabling the children to look in at the world they already inhabited. Their small hands could reach through to lay breakfast, and move the chairs for extra guests. The roof hinged back so their bedrooms were a free-for-all. Only one room was harder to explore, and so they missed the arguments, the toll taken by the hours the encyclopædic venture had incurred. He blew, and watched clumps of dust drifting through memory's build. He could still feel the rasp of the saw through the ply, still smell the paint taking so long to dry as Christmas morning came around.

*

Occasionally, when he hung out washing between the hedge and the barn, and it flapped into the laurels, loud as a sudden pigeon, a shirt or skirt would billow loose and fall to the grass, and as he re-pegged it he would think of the full day's exploit and soiling that the action implied: it reminded him of his wife, when she wrote on the old typewriter, batting the carriage back to its start when she wanted a new line, and how, when something went awry, she would wrench the sheet of paper from the roller and let it drop to the floor before scrolling in another, giving her lost idea another chance. Not his wife of these past thirty years; another wife, who might have written poems.

Spiders

You remove my glasses,
easing the pain in the bridge
of my nose where the metal
frame has cut through skin
and left a rusty line.
'Is that a *stitch*?'
The bulbous machine

>glides towards me
>and I rest my unshaven chin
>on a bed of tissues.
>You sit to one side and shine
>a pencil-thin torch-
>beam into the small
>black hole

to strike up
black forked lightning—a map
of veins like crazed pottery,
cartoon trees...
'Fighting spiders,' you say
before you fire
a puff of air

>straight at my eye,
>testing for glaucoma.
>It makes me cry.
>With one hand you stretch
>my eyelids apart,
>leaving me no option
>but to watch

your fingertip closing in,
placing the transparent petal
in the drift of my tears
with such intimate touch,
turning it until it
settles and my vision
clears.

> 'Which is brightest,
> the red or the green?'
> 'They look... to be honest
> I haven't had much sleep.'
> You slide and pluck the lens away
> between finger and thumb.
> 'Now, you try.'

Brideshead Revisited

I stand where Jeremy Irons
would smoke a cigarette,
my poems acting as captions
for photographs of the estate.
A tourist asks me how I cope

with Lord Sebastian in a mope
or drunk and I tell him a twisted
version of the truth—
something to be going along with.

A Speckled Hen

When Rosalind, Countess of Carlisle
discovered temperance,
the Castle's supply of Audit Ale
was poured down the drains,

though for every story of every bottle
of finest claret dumped in the lake,
another gives them to a hospital,
or reckons that no dipsomaniac

would have touched them, the wine
so foul, the corks like fungus,
with Rosalind—a speckled hen—
still flitting among us

like a ghost, refusing to elucidate:
I go barefoot, barefoot, barefoot!

Blackbird

A high-speed clunk into toughened glass—a decade thick, but I can still feel the tremors. Poor thing, swooping from cherry tree towards the moors—through the barn where thin air used to hold sway, only a rusting red tractor to negotiate. I scooped his dark, slumped shape with a shovel, pondering: how strange that the thud of sudden death should live longer, travel further...

A Betrothal

Old wives will claim credit
for her running into the field
to share her joyous news
but the murder of crows
had the wherewithal

to fly with it,
their raucous echoes
tearing at her proffered vows
to see if they would yield.

Fire

On Egdon Heath

He lies in a bed of crisping bracken—bracken straight out of the book he's discarded in the sun. He takes a magnifying glass from his pocket, focuses on the crinkled fronds. A half-hidden lizard squirms at the intrusion that grows to a torrid inquisition. He senses the power he has to ratchet up the heat into a crime. His own skin is darkening. Unread pages of the novel begin their incendiary curl.

Fahrenheit 451

One toy in particular he remembers, motoring over the carpet, with a yellow ladder you could wind as high as... as high as the TV... its astonishing feat to reverse from every collision—with chair leg, skirting board, coal scuttle, cat—and set off on a new mission... in the age when everyone—much as they needed rescuing—seemed safe. There it is, still wound up, or battered, he can't remember which, nosing into trouble and saving the day. Bright red, like in a film...

1 February 1829

His brother might have painted it, a scene of damnation, but he—he wanted his hellfire more real. He sat through evensong, fingering the razor in his pocket, sick of the priests' buzzing nonsense in his ear, then hid in the bell-tower until dark: shredded the velvet in the Bishop's pew; piled it high with cushions and hymn books and set it alight. Grabbing a bell-rope, he swung through the minster window like a cartoon. And yes, they found him, tramping to the pub, fragments of flint and stained glass in his pockets—but he was adamant: *Not me, my lord, but my God is guilty.*

Visionary

Some nights, by the hearth, he thought he saw blue-green phantoms within the flames. And one morning, sitting in the big bay window of his parents' room, when they were elsewhere (where?), he watched a hummingbird come to the glass, its frantic wings—like blurred rainbows—enabling it to hang, poised in the air... but he lived on the wrong continent, no one believed him, and later, when his mind wasn't right, he wondered if that had been the case all along, that he'd been seeing things. The thought torched his world like a burning bush.

Firebreak

He's desperate to beat the clock, to outsmart the wobbling air that is everywhere, loitering like an arrogant accomplice. He clears the undergrowth, deadwood and detritus, ploughing the ground to rip out the dregs of anything combustible—the spine of a notebook, a bloodstained dress, anything that a single blown ember might decide is something other than pure dirt—to form a corridor in the bush, wide as a landing strip where nothing, ever, will be welcome to land. Lightning's prophecy won't come close. But fire... fire is there where he least thinks to look: in the eyes of his dog, head on paws in the shade beside his truck—the very same deadpan stare from when he built a gate too high to be jumped. Or so he thought.

The Nest

After she left, his magnum opus became a greater obsession. Blowtorch in hand, he scraped the melting cream paint from the delicate curves of every banister, then sanded them to perfection. In his study, the walls were measured, drilled, plugged, and finally lined with thick bookshelves that could never sag. One day there'd be a bathroom. Meanwhile, the garden ran wild. Nettles, head high, encroached on the windows. Forcing his way into the shed, he reached past the redundant mower for more radical gear, slung the heavy tank of gas over his shoulder and let rip, a wallop of flame razing the chaos. How he saw the pheasant's nest in time, he still can't say. The stubborn hen quivered in the heat, her dozen eggs hidden from view; he crouched in the strangely amplified silence, and stared into her eye.

Dusk

One evening he sat looking across the valley. He'd cleaned out the rusty iron pot-bellied stove that had collected water from weeks of summer rain, cleaned out the crunchy wet charcoal mess, and lit a fire. Bats were on their haphazard orbits around the laurels by the barn. The sky began to burn as night air cooled. Leaves turned to black, and blood-red ladybirds harboured within their gloom became dark-star dewdrops anticipating dawn. He felt the stretch of past and future squeezing the present into oblivion.

Millennial

The village feast had become a tired re-enactment. Then, that year, the corner-shop box of tricks went global. We gathered round a bonfire, with hot dogs and beer, handing out sparklers. The children's crocodile gloves fizzed and flickered at the mouth, strange words glittering in the air. On the hillside opposite, further small glimmerings took up the narrative of the night, and I thought of those older conflagrations of faggots and furze, imagined *Rainbarrow* as one of the words lingering like coppery fireflies—and later, as the children slept, still dancing in their eyes.

Christmas

When everyone else had tired, when the uneaten mince pies were packed away, and even the dog had called it a day, he would turn out all the other lights and sit alone, in perfect silence, staring at the lamp-lit tree—its constructed beauty: baubles and tinsel perfectly arranged; his daughters' ideas so evident in the scintillating mix. Then came the moment he himself would have to move. For twelve nights he wondered if he could do it at all; for twelve nights he delayed the moment ever longer, pondering his own grip on a world in which a tree had most to say. He finally flicked the switch and snuffed the candle on the cast iron range, sending black into black.

The New Slip Inn/The Pub with No Beer

Walking home past the village church, I'm drawn
to the lamplit window in the cottage
opposite, the old blacksmith's—before that
a pub: The New Slip Inn. (How come, this far
from a waterway?) The interior
is bedecked with memorabilia
that materialise, hammer and tongs
in the glow from a fire, wooden bellows
pumping the vision into life. Then it
cools, but somehow softens. It has the feel
of something dimly remembered, windows
opened in an old calendar. I lean
in to put right one of the slipped horseshoes
that has spilled its luck, making the world turn

upside down. I've passed through a cupboard door
and walked out onto a bleached veranda,
not that of my own childhood but one where
another family has assembled
for a shot outside The Pub with No Beer—
except the father has a glass of it.
He rests his forearms on the railing while
his son twists awkwardly bored, and mother
stands back in her sunnies. You, on the edge
of your new beauty, smile to camera,
a little white dog between your bare feet.
You're already telling me that the song's
what this is all about: Old Billy, a
blacksmith; how and when the warrigals called.

Midsummer

Twenty-eight years after you were born
I come home to a garden so overgrown,
so summer-lush in the afternoon sun
it's a green hallucination

        where you sit in the shade of new lime trees,
                your one-year-old eyes
      fixed on a sponge cake printed with strawberries

        and at your side, with sprawling pink tongue
           that follows your every move, *the wrong
        dog entirely*—memory's mistuned song

through which we marvel at the beyond.
We take turns to dip our blind
fingers into the box of fine grey sand
and let loose grains of the past into the wind.

In a Country Churchyard

It's late afternoon when I push the gate
and manoeuvre in the heavy mower.
Thirty years here, I'm still a newcomer
but there are names I recognise as well
as the next man: Foster, Duncan, Goodwill,
Robert and Molly Harding, and Lorna—
Lorna Lee, at whose grave my strong but frail
memory trembles, so that I lose all
grip and the engine cuts out... Her heart
had that same problem; for the infection
in her leg she suffered amputation
unanæsthetised. O what a feeble
thing, by comparison, at which to fail:
to mow the churchyard grass; or worse, to write.

1768

I think of Laurence Sterne
on the anatomy table
the same year someone
collects Elizabeth Rainbow
from the foundling hospital.

Neither could know
of their multiple burials
or how many skulls or souls
might suffer the same fate.

Country House Visitor, c.1996

He woke to a morning perfectly still:
a lazy mist rising in the garden;
a grey heron poised at the water's edge,
intent. He slipped quietly downstairs to plunge,
naked, into the over-heated pool.

Later, he kept returning to the scene:
how she blundered in, armed with a towel
not wanting though to linger but to urge
him on his way; how he felt such a fool
as he threw his bag into the car, turned

on the gravel drive and saw the heron
lift, stall and sprawl—just as he heard the gun—
legs hanging slack like electric cable,
sparks of bright blood flumping into the pond.

Steadicam

TRACKING SHOT. INTERIOR.
Danny, pedaling in the corridor
of the Overlook Hotel, the only sound
the rumble of wheels, muffled
by carpet. CUT TO: EXTERIOR:

Danny, placing one foot after another
into his own snow-hollow prints...
backwards... no room for error...
his life in the balance.

All work and no play

Clattering through the lobby—
the quick-action strikes
of a repetitive axe
whittling your self to a stack
of fractional mistakes: Jakc

a... dlllboy... this your hobby—
battering out these indented
letters on the page, demented
as any splintering affray.

redruM

Their naked bodies, kneeling
in secular prayer, were shadows
playing on the wall,
but turning
his head he saw the full

technicolour act for what it was,
crudely overwritten in thick
strokes of scarlet lipstick
on the sliding mirror doors.

Macbeth
GSP Studios, Bubwith, Yorkshire, June 2016

Lady Macduff, so beautiful, so young, is delaying proceedings; it's her first day, she's worried about her hair. There are whispers... Another ten minutes. Someone puts a red cross on the far, green wall. Thick wires spill from the camera. Finally, she reappears, her hair the same perfection it was before. I want to tell her how little it matters, but my presence means nothing. It's as if I'm not there.

*

We adjourn for lunch in a grassy courtyard. There's a net, strung between the two barns where everyone sleeps. Fleance has found a playmate, and flicks the shuttlecock up towards the sun. It speeds from his raquet, then stalls. The breeze is against him, and as the shuttlecock falls into the net, then falls again, his friend losing patience, I have to keep telling myself that it's just a game.

*

As I drive away, I catch a glimpse of Macbeth in his leather skirts, standing in the middle of the country lane to catch a signal. He waves one hand in the air as he talks, perhaps to his wife; the other is clutched to the side of his head, and I imagine the blood from his ear now smeared on his mobile. The sun is out. The roof is back and I hear clear birdsong above the engine's hum and the rubbery grind of tyres through the dust. Trees in full leaf rush towards me on both sides.

*

The pall bearers heave the draped corpse to their shoulders, then wait, while people stare at the geometry on screen, pointing fingers. Faces, now familiar, form a corridor through which the body must pass. The Macbeths, at the head of the lines, lean in to share a secret joke. The children look nervous. Someone adjusts the fall of the cloth, asks one line of mourners to move in: six inches. More. Stop. Now there's a perfect vanishing point. A bell rings. The cortège begins its slow, slow shuffle. The screen is toggled from green to black.

*

There are some with very little to do. Really very little. The First Murderer, for instance: next to nothing. Four weeks in and his whiskied nights have grown into whiskied days. He's no longer good company. And his face—his face now looks bruised from within, and the ever-blackening bags under his eyes are carrying a sickness. But this morning, as he hauls his self-brutalised body from his bed, he's finally summoned, and the method in his madness uncoils like a snake. He's sharp, word-perfect, dressed to kill.

*

Life intervenes; death, rather. We wait in the boxed pews, with organ music faintly out of tune. In the front row, grandchildren, generations adrift from the white-haired assembly behind them. As the tributes begin, I think of the absent body, burnt or buried months ago. I think of the dummy carried from Dunsinane under a grey cloth. I hear a sound that could be the soft popping of a microphone, that is actually raindrops falling through the defective lead of the Coxwold church roof. I think of tomorrow: Banquo's ghost. We adjourn to the inevitable feast.

*

At the wrap party, Lady Macbeth is back on top form, serving the squid, and telling everyone how her father would pop their eyes with his thumbs, then strip out the spine, and deal with the ink. Macduff clearly finds this some kind of turn-on, while Banquo winces; he's had a skinful already and looks set to pass out. The Porter, who bided his time for the whole six weeks—almost written out of the action—is pissing into an ice bucket. The director, exhausted before the evening began, is finding a second wind. He knocks back a tumbler of Talisker, then another, and thinks there might be a film in all this. But where's Macbeth? Where the fuck is Macbeth?

Four Poster

The frame was hung with tapestries. If he lay
on the bed and stretched his arms and legs
towards the corners he could almost imagine
a quartering of himself, a bloody severance

*

and what possessed her ? the time she scattered
rose petals in between the sheets, so that when
they regained their senses they also reeled
from the crimson stains that suggested a gross

*

bereavement, and since none of the four
children could house the legacy whole, the bed
was dismembered, the individual, equal limbs
allotted to separate homes, like orphans,

*

this one drilled for a red and black flex to run
through its hollowed mahogany core
like an artery, powering the electric light
where I sit at night and witness its first flickers.

Fractures

The pub shut down; neighbourly disagreements
went to ground. Now, at harvest, rifts
rehearse their muscular subterranean flux
with ice-cold wine in the old schoolhouse, farmers

*

who needs them—and that soft-spoken gardener
is the one who stole the ten-year woodpile
from your field. You seriously consider
setting fire to his house as a form of poetic

*

impotence was what the solicitor called it
when news of his wife's affair was forcibly planted
in his brain. He calmly took his gun and shot her
dog, which was the final straw, the whole village

*

divided in its outrage, mouthing off words
that were all too connived, debased, toxic; a body
politic reeling from some seismic blow job,
its blind eye not knowing which way to turn.

For Sale: Number 453

I drive past the nondescript house,
remembering how ten years back
it was made infamous;
how I came to the roadblock
and matched it to the manhunt

unfolding in the news. I try to forget
the hogtied detail, the blunt
instruments of recall; take note
instead of that newly planted tree.

The Bulmer Murder

The story of Captain John Bolton of Bulmer, near Castle Howard, accused of murdering Elizabeth Rainbow, his apprentice girl, a single woman, at the parish of Bulmer in the county of York on the 21st day of August, 1774.

Sunday, 21st of March, 2008

I was shifting a barrow
of earth across the garden
to relieve one clog of land
and replenish another.
The wind had got up,
and with it the strange
swift tilt of time:

> the familiar low sun
> of late afternoon; the sky
> thickening with layers
> of black, the backdrop
> for a bending spectrum
> of light—a double rainbow
> ghosting itself

into the garish orange
of pantiled roof
and the electric green
of wet, lit grass;
the whole village
coloured like the glass
windows of its church.

I had stumbled
on your story, the burden
of that barrow suddenly
forcing my hand.
A troubled sunset bled
its deepening red
into my eye.

A month later, 1774

  ELIZABETH SCAYLING. *What age was Elizabeth Rainbow?*—*I cannot tell ; but ſhe has lived with him for ſix or ſeven years : When ſhe came to him ſhe was a little girl, about eight or ten years old.*
  JANE TAYLOR *(neighbour). I ſaid what did ſhe ail ; ſhe ſaid ſhe could not tell, but her legs ſwelled ; her miſtreſs was in the hall and heard us, and ſaid if ſhe was well to eat and work, there could be little the matter with her... She ſaid that when Mr Bolton or her went to York they muſt get ſomething for her, but ſhe was ſo ſtupid ſhe would not take it, though they got it. I thought it was the green-ſickneſs.*
  THOMAS BUSFIELD *(journeyman to Mr Garenclers, apothecary, York). He [John Bolton] wanted an electuary making up, for which he had a preſcription... a preparation of ſteel... for removing obſtructions... dangerous to be given to a woman with child.*

21st of August

Soon after three o'clock,
around the time that Cook
sails west of Pentecost
in the South Pacific,
Captain Bolton
sees his wife off to Foston
for tea with a friend.

      The Bowes boy
      is next, on an errand
      to Stittenham. It's a plan,
      surely, to have everyone
      out of the way,
      though perhaps for no more
      than the scheduled misdemeanour

of habitual adultery;
Betty his apprentice
in those breathless arts
of which nobody speaks.
What then happened
to press his hand
into something worse

      than 'crime of passion'
      could possibly suggest;
      abominable, gross?
      Even the speculation hurts.
      What hours of cruelty
      had turned into weeks?
      What did she resist?

5 o'clock

EMANUEL BOWES. *When I got back... I turned the mare loofe in the yard, and went to the glafs door that opens into the orchard. I lift up the latch and found it faft... I went round to the ftreet door and knocked for near a quarter of an hour. William Mafterman, who lives oppofite, was fitting at his door with a child on his knee...*

WILLIAM MASTERMAN. *I laugh'd at him and faid, knock, 'Manuel, thy name's up (an old faying in our town). I then faw [Bolton] walking acrofs the yard, from the glafs-door towards the ftable.*

EMANUEL BOWES. *[My mafter] was very much in a flutter; his hair stood upon end, and he had not his hat on... his face was much heated, and looked very red... He bid me... go to the Moor-houfes... I was to go to Robert Boys about fome hay. When I came back... [my master] was fet by the fire in the parlour, drinking tea. He faid Emanuel, did you meet Betty on the road; and I faid No, have you fent her an errand; he faid fhe is run away... He faid while he came out at the glafs door to tell me to go to the Moor-houfes, fhe went out at the ftreet door, and ran away, and he faw no more of her. I went into the kitchen. There was no Betty there. I fat about half an hour, it was then time to go to milk.*

WILLIAM MASTERMAN. *[The ftreet-door] never was opened all that time. I am very certain nobody came out till fix o'clock when I went away.*

Earlier that day, 2014

I walk the two miles
to where you sent him, Bowes,
matching my every footstep
to the topography of the crime,
wondering where it was
that the cow doctor resided
as I struggle enough to find

        the two bed & breakfasts
        for our imminent guests.
        How was there time
        to dismantle a rainbow,
        consign the colours of a life
        into dirt? You can see
        directly from one hilltop

to the other—how a bonfire
might send its semaphore
of flame
across the valley,
its contours clouded
with an outback haze of flies
like documentary malingerers

        wanting to know
        how each passing year
        and every underhand
        second
        becomes an accomplice
        to the illusion of proof;
        becomes proof.

Monday, 22nd of August, 1774

EMANUEL BOWES. *I got my breakfaſt about nine o'clock. My maſter came to me, and said, 'Manwell, you muſt get your ſpade, I have a job for you. I was to carry it into the orchard, and he would mark out the place where I was to take the earth. He ordered me to fill the wheel-barrow ; and I ſaw him lay the boards for the barrow to run through the hall to the cellar door ; I ſaw him throw the earth from the barrow into the cellar... he gave me the barrow to take back, and get ſome more ; he told me to throw it in at the cellar door and it fell down the ſteps ; when I had got about half a dozen barrow-fulls, I heard ſomebody in the cellar moving the dirt ; I kept wheeling on for about half a dozen more, about twelve in all. I wheeled every morning for a fortnight together...*

Main Street, September, 1983

When I first set foot
through the front door
I found the kitchen sink
full of muddy water
as if someone had rinsed
the filth from their boots
and left the evidence

        as a dismal welcome.
        I couldn't but wonder
        at the nonchalance—
        like Bolton's, feet up
        by the fire after his labour,
        drinking his tea,
        then resting over a gate

three yards from his house,
calling to a neighbour
about some wood.
How did he look?—as *free
and hearty as ever I ſaw him
in my life.*
A few days later

    he had the guts
    to be back—the vendor,
    thinking he could chop
    more logs and set off
    on a rant—kick up a stink
    about townies convinced
    they owned the damn place.

Priſoner's defence

    JOHN BOLTON. *My reaſon for filling up the cellar was, that the water came in very faſt ever ſince it had been ſunk, which is near nine years ago : It came in ſo faſt that it hurt the foundation of the houſe, and part of it, at that end, fell in about two or three years ago. In the winter before laſt, my eldeſt ſon fell into it, when it was full of water, which made Mrs Bolton and myſelf ſo uneaſy, that I promiſed I would fill it up as ſoon as the cellar was dry. This declaration I made to ſeveral perſons ; and as ſoon as the cellar was dry, and hay-time over, I ſet about it, by giving directions to the lad, and telling him that he ſhould have the gardener to aſſiſt him...*

Now

When the water rises,
or I dig again, believing
there might come to light
some residual trace
of your act—a faint pigment
in the soil, a fragment
of bone or a microscopic hair

>of rope—I catch the echo
>of whatever melody
>once played on that fife
>before it was put
>to its gruesome last use.
>It's the same birdsong
>fills the evening air

as when you gathered
the lambs into your fold.
I listen and pick out
a tune on the piano
to redeem not your deed
but the tools of its trade:
the fife, the cord, the spade.

>The tune is a *courante*:
>she'd run away before;
>you clung to the fantasy
>that absolving your lies
>she had done it once more;
>all that grim stuff
>of your hiding concealed.

5th of September, 1774

JOHN HALL. *When I went down the steps, they appeared like a slope bank with fresh earth... one corner [of the cellar] was filled with fresh earth within a little of the chamber joists...*

MARK RICHARDSON. *I took the shovel, and took a little of the earth, and found a stick. I gave it a pull, but found it fast. I gave it a twist, and it broke. I saw some hair, and then I perceived her left arm, which seemed fast. I then took my dig and pulled her up. Her arms were tied behind her back. There was a cord around her neck, and the other part of the fife was twisted in the cord, and tied under her left arm. I knew her before but she was very much altered; her face was very much swollen, and of a blue colour.*

JOHN HALL. *We picked carefully about with his shovel and discovered her head.*

JOSEPH WEST (surgeon). *When I opened the body, I found a male foetus. About five months. I took off [the rope]. It was twice about, and twisted with the fife. I examined the gullet with my finger, and found it twisted in two.*

(undated)

Did you picture yourself
cohabiting with the dead?
You and your wife
with your child and lover
gagged forever
in the improvised graveyard
mere inches underfoot?

       Or did you know you would flee
       with a brace of pistols
       and the family silver
       bulging from your clothes,
       ready to buy your way
       to new trouble, new strife?
       I pretend it was me

with disintegrating victim,
sentenced for the term
of my natural life.
It's not hard to feel—
even from the other side
of the world—
the terrifying seal

       of my lips as I doff my hat
       to familiar strangers,
       pass the time of day
       with the comfort of untold
       manageable dangers;
       a dumb beast aware
       at least of others in my care.

27th of March, 1775

THE HON. SIR HENRY GOULD, KNIGHT *(His Majesty's Justice of the Court of Common Pleas). The law has thought fit in great wisdom to inflict a punishment upon persons found guilty of a crime of this nature, which points out the heinousness of the offence. This will happen when you are no more in this world. Consider with yourself and endeavour to find mercy, while there are any hopes of it. There is very little time for you to live in this world, but if you employ that time properly, you may find mercy from the Fountain of all mercies.*

The sentence that the law obliges me to pronounce upon you is, That you, John Bolton, be led from this place from whence you came, and taken to the place of execution on Wednesday morning, and hung by the neck till you are dead; and after that your body to be dissected and anatomized. God have mercy upon your soul!

Twilight, late millennium

What made me copy
this account of the trial
into my own dull-boy hand?
It became like a memory,
translating the poor facts
in all their muddied clarity
from sixpenny pamphlet

> into my new
> yellow notebook,
> every detail
> a fresh smudge
> verging on the bland;
> a discrepancy that distracts.
> And then?

What more to do
with the raw material
than idly retrace each
shape on the page,
allowing the *r*s to curl
over into *n*s and bear
witness to *Murder*

> twisting into *Munden*,
> feeling the whole gamut
> of fear in my stomach;
> the arrhythmic thump
> of my drifting heart;
> the concomitant lump
> in my throat.

POSTSCRIPT. *During his trial, he behaved with a degree of boldneſs and unconcern, ſeldom to be diſcovered in perſons under ſuch circumſtances ; but when the cords and fife, with which the unfortunate girl was ſtrangled, were produced, his countenance fell, and he ſeemed greatly agitated. After the judge had ſolemly pronounced ſentence upon him he perſevered in his declaration, ſaying, in a manner that ſeemed to ſhock the whole court, by G–d, my lord, I am innocent.*

The next morning he was attended by two clergymen, and ſtill perſiſted in aſſerting that he was innocent ; they obſerved to him, that he had ſhocked the whole court, not only with the declaration of his innocence, but alſo with the manner in which he expreſſed it, which was foreign to the character he aſſumed : After having repeatedly conjured him to cloſe the ſcene with that behaviour becoming a ſincere penitent, they had the concern to leave him as they found him, obdurate.

Early on Wedneſday morning he found means to be his own executioner in the cell. He effected this, by tying a liſt garter and a piece of cord that ſupported his irons to a handkerchief, the end of which he had fixed to a piece of wood, broke off from an old table in the cell, and put it through an air-hole : He was diſcovered between ſix and ſeven o'clock hanged, or rather ſtrangled, his feet being on the ground. The body was not cold. A ſurgeon was immediately ſent for, who open'd a vein, and he bled a little, but was too far gone to be recovered.

The coroner's inqueſt ſat upon the body, and brought in their verdict,

felo de ſe.

Canberra, 1st of October, 2016

Afterword

I owe the impetus for this work to colleagues at the University of Canberra, and in particular Paul Hetherington, who initiated two collaborative projects, the first writing prose poems, the second 'unruly sonnets'. Both forms were new to my own practice and proved immensely useful in pursuing a number of themes and subjects I had had in mind for many years.

Researching other adaptations of the sonnet form led me to Oliver Reynolds' 'Seven little sonnets on Frederick the Great' (1987). The idea of the 'miniature' sonnet—going beyond Gerard Manley Hopkins' 'Curtal Sonnets' (1918), in a five- and four-line stanza structure, enabled many slight or subsidiary ideas to gain some formal strength.

Longer structures also emerged, including sonnet sequences, and poems where paired stanzas—each of seven lines and with rhyme working loosely across the whole—became a new, natural form of expression.

The overarching theme, and preoccupation of these poems, is the role of the accomplice—particularly as manifested in the poetic biography, or non-fiction poetry as it is sometimes described. This branch of life writing is widespread, and yet not fully recognised within the field of creative non-fiction generally. Not everything presented here of course, though, is factual.

Much of the work focuses on a small area of North Yorkshire (close to Castle Howard) with which I am closely acquainted, but the perspective is from Australia. As Janet Frame asserts, 'All writers are exiles' (1987), and geographical distance has perhaps both driven and enhanced the gaze.

Works Cited

Frame, J. (1987) *The Envoy from Mirror City*, London: Paladin
Hopkins, G. M. (1918) *Poems*, London: Humphrey Milford
Reynolds, O. (1987) *The Player Queen's Wife*, London: Faber & Faber

Notes

Rat Tales
The opening section is taken from *Straw Dogs* (dir. Sam Peckinpah, 1971); the closing section from *The Tale of Samuel Whiskers or The Roly-Poly Pudding*, by Beatrix Potter (Frederick Warne & Co., 1908).

Brideshead Revisited
The Granada Television adaptation of Evelyn Waugh's 1945 novel was filmed at Castle Howard, North Yorkshire, and screened in 1980.

A Speckled Hen
Rosalind Howard (1845–1921) became Countess of Carlisle and mistress of Castle Howard in 1888. She was president of the World Women's Temperance Association.

Fire
Jonathan Martin (brother of the painter John Martin) set fire to York Minster on 1 February 1829.

The New Slip Inn/The Pub with No Beer
The beerless pub referenced is the Taylors Arm Hotel, NSW, where songwriter Gordon Parsons 'acquired' Dan Sheahan's 1943 poem based on the Day Dawn Hotel, QLD. Slim Dusty's 1957 recording made it famous. The New Slip Inn, Bulmer, was demolished and replaced by the blacksmith's shop in the early 1900s.

1768
Laurence Sterne is believed to have been buried three times: twice at Hanover Square in London, 1768, and finally in Coxwold, 1969. Elizabeth Rainbow was one of many young people taken from Ackworth Hospital, West Yorkshire, (a branch of the Foundling Hospital in London) as 'apprentices'. Following abuse of this system, the hospital closed in 1773.

Steadicam, All work and no play, redruM
Stanley Kubrick's film, *The Shining*, based on Stephen King's novel, was released in 1980.

Macbeth
Kit Monkman's film adaptation of *Macbeth* is scheduled for release in 2017.

The Bulmer Murder
The italicised text is taken from *The Trial at Large of John Bolton, Gent.*, printed by N. Nickson in Blake Street, York.

Acknowledgements

Journals:
Rabbit
Stride
Uneven Floor
Westerly

Anthologies:
Seam: Prose Poetry Project (IPSI, 2015)
Pulse: Prose Poems (Recent Work Press, 2016)

Exhibitions:
The Encyclopædia of Forgotten Things (Belconnen Arts Centre, 2016)
Beauties and Beasts (Belconnen Arts Centre, 2017)

The 'Keys' and 'Fire' poems were first published within chapbooks under the Authorised Theft imprint.

Paul Munden is Postdoctoral Research Fellow at the University of Canberra, where he is also Program Manager for the International Poetry Studies Institute (IPSI). He is General Editor of *Writing in Education* and *Writing in Practice*, both published by the National Association of Writers in Education (NAWE), of which he is Director. He was reader for Stanley Kubrick from 1988–98. He has worked as conference poet for the British Council and edited *Feeling the Pressure: Poetry and science of climate change* (British Council, 2008). His collection of poems, *Asterisk* (Smith/Doorstop, 2011), is based on Shandy Hall, former home of Laurence Sterne. *Analogue/Digital*, a volume of his new and selected poems was published by Smith/Doorstop in 2015. He has lived in Bulmer, North Yorkshire, for over 30 years, now dividing his time with work in Canberra.

2016 Editions

Pulse Prose Poetry Project
Incantations Subhash Jaireth
Transit Niloofar Fanaiyan
Gallery of Antique Art Paul Hetherington
Sentences from the Archive Jen Webb
River's Edge Owen Bullock

2017 Editions

A Song, the World to Come Miranda Lello
Cities: Ten Cities, Ten Poets Various
The Bulmer Murder Paul Munden
Dew and Broken Glass Penny Drysdale
Members Only Melinda Smith and Caren Florance
the future, un-imagine Angela Gardner and Caren Florance
Proof Maggie Shapley
Soap Charlotte Guest
Isolator Monica Carroll
Icarus Paul Hetherington
Work & Play Owen Bullock

all titles available from
www.recentworkpress.com

RECENT
WORK
PRESS

Lightning Source UK Ltd.
Milton Keynes UK
UKOW08f1527010517
300263UK00002B/70/P